YOUR KNOWLEDGE HAS VALUE

- We will publish your bachelor's and master's thesis, essays and papers

- Your own eBook and book - sold worldwide in all relevant shops

- Earn money with each sale

Upload your text at www.GRIN.com
and publish for free

Bibliographic information published by the German National Library:

The German National Library lists this publication in the National Bibliography; detailed bibliographic data are available on the Internet at http://dnb.dnb.de .

This book is copyright material and must not be copied, reproduced, transferred, distributed, leased, licensed or publicly performed or used in any way except as specifically permitted in writing by the publishers, as allowed under the terms and conditions under which it was purchased or as strictly permitted by applicable copyright law. Any unauthorized distribution or use of this text may be a direct infringement of the author s and publisher s rights and those responsible may be liable in law accordingly.

Imprint:

Copyright © 2017 GRIN Verlag, Open Publishing GmbH
Print and binding: Books on Demand GmbH, Norderstedt Germany
ISBN: 9783668473676

This book at GRIN:

http://www.grin.com/en/e-book/369020/student-learning-styles-and-second-language-acquisition

Alfhonce Michael

Student learning styles and second language acquisition

A brief overview of recent studies

GRIN - Your knowledge has value

Since its foundation in 1998, GRIN has specialized in publishing academic texts by students, college teachers and other academics as e-book and printed book. The website www.grin.com is an ideal platform for presenting term papers, final papers, scientific essays, dissertations and specialist books.

Visit us on the internet:

http://www.grin.com/

http://www.facebook.com/grincom

http://www.twitter.com/grin_com

Student learning styles and second language acquisition

Contents

Student learning styles and second language acquisition 2

    Piper, T. (2011). And then there were two: Children and second language learning. Toronto: Pippin Pub. 2

    Purpura, J. E. (January 01, 2016). Second and Foreign Language Assessment. *The Modern Language Journal, 100,* 190-208. 2

    Georgetown University Round Table on Languages and Linguistics, & Alatis, J. E. (2010). *Linguistics, language teaching, and language acquisition: The interdependence of theory, practice, and research.* Washington, D.C: Georgetown University Press. 3

    Griffiths, C., & İnceçay, G. (June 01, 2016). Styles and Style-Stretching: How are They Related to Successful Learning?. *Journal of Psycholinguistic Research, 45,* 3, 599-613..... 3

    Mirzaee, S., & Maftoon, P. (December 01, 2016). An examination of Vygotsky's socio-cultural theory in second language acquisition: the role of higher order thinking enhancing techniques and the EFL learners' use of private speech in the construction of reasoning. *Asian-pacific Journal of Second and Foreign Language Education, 1,* 1, 1-25. 4

    VanPatten, B., & Williams, J. (2015). *Theories in second language acquisition: An introduction.* New York : Routledge 4

    Butler, Y. G., & Hakuta, K. (January 01, 2008). Bilingualism and Second Language Acquisition. 114-144. 5

    Brown, H. D. (2007). *Principles of language learning and teaching.* White Plains, NY: Pearson Longman. 5

    Leaver, B. L., Ehrman, M. E., & Shekhtman, B. (2005). *Achieving success in second language acquisition.* Cambridge, UK: Cambridge University Press. 6

    Haywood, A. L. (2005). The relationship between student learning styles and L2 acquisition in two international high schools' english language classrooms in Jeddah, Saudi Arabia. Thesis (Ph. D.): University of Mississippi 6

    Zhonggen, Y. (April 01, 2016). The Impact of the E-Collaborative and Traditional Learning Styles on Learning Outcomes and Anxiety. *International Journal of E-Collaboration (ijec), 12,* 2, 27-47. 7

References 7

Student learning styles and second language acquisition

This is hereby a sensible process where one learns of another language than of his or her first language. This process takes place after one has already gained the first language. Therefore, when studying the second language the learner can also find the language to be the third, forth or fifth in his or her studies. The first language is the first language a person learns immediately after he or she is born. Caregivers or parents that surround an individual when he or she is born mostly teach this language. Like the second language, learning one can also have more than one language at the same time.

Piper, T. (2011). And then there were two: Children and second language learning. Toronto: Pippin Pub.

The author looks at the different forms of learning both first and second language. He indicates that for an individual to learn a foreign language or a second language it will be a great success whereas if one studies the first language there will not be much success considered to the others. The research study on second language acquisition clarifies how students differ from each other when acquiring a second language and explains how alike the students are. According to the author, student-learning languages disagree in terms of some factors like affective variables, learning strategies, demographic variables, and learning style in spite of the common language and memory and cognitive processing in the brain (Piper, 2011). In addition, these factors have reflective effects on the success of the student by assisting them on how they will approach the learning task in the language.

Purpura, J. E. (January 01, 2016). Second and Foreign Language Assessment. *The Modern Language Journal, 100,* **190-208.**

The article discusses the different concept applied in understanding the languages whereby one can understand that for a teacher to create better way of learning for the learners he or she should acquire information of how the learners take their studies (Purpura, 2016).

One can understand the difficult system of language teaching and learning if she or he is able to access knowledge about personality's differences. For a student to achieves and approaches second language learning this study assist by exploring one of the factors that distinguish one student from the other.

Georgetown University Round Table on Languages and Linguistics, & Alatis, J. E. (2010). *Linguistics, language teaching, and language acquisition: The interdependence of theory, practice, and research.* **Washington, D.C: Georgetown University Press.**

The book lays emphasis on the different language strategies and the manner in which they are effective for the teachers and the students. According to the authors, t is very important in critical performance of the language when taking strategies in language learning. When learning this language there are six strategies that are involved which include the following cognitive, memory, metacognitive, affective or social, and comprehensive. Therefore, it is necessary for ones strategies to differ other person's strategies (Georgetown University Round Table on Languages and Linguistics & Alatis, 2010). Within the cognitive model of learning language, learning strategies can be described effectively.

Griffiths, C., & İnceçay, G. (June 01, 2016). Styles and Style-Stretching: How are They Related to Successful Learning?. *Journal of Psycholinguistic Research, 45,* **3, 599-613.**

The authors introduce the readers to the cognitive form of study. A person who follows cognitive strategy is able to reason out things and analyze it. According to the cognitive model of learning, it suggests that learning is a dynamic and active process whereby students get the opportunities to organize their information, retain what is essential to them, and reflect on their success effort of learning, using appropriately the information and from their surrounding selecting information. Learning enables the use of three cognitive theories, which include the long-term theory, short-term theory and working memory (Griffiths & İnceçay, 2016). From the long-term theory, one is able to store information that comes from education and personal experience, while short-term theory enables an individual to recall information that comparatively insignificant.

Mirzaee, S., & Maftoon, P. (December 01, 2016). An examination of Vygotsky's sociocultural theory in second language acquisition: the role of higher order thinking enhancing techniques and the EFL learners' use of private speech in the construction of reasoning. *Asian-pacific Journal of Second and Foreign Language Education, 1,* **1, 1-25.**

The article talks of the different theories in learning language which includes working memory whereby the information in the memory is manipulated. The reason why the strategies are being used is that they have a prominent way in the application of the cognitive view applied in learning as underlying learning and thinking process. In order to aid the system of information processing it is suggested that the working memory is where the student strategies are positioned. It is also necessary for one to exert control over the deployment to assist in managing the resources (Mirzaee & Maftoon, 2016). Sensible mental activity is required in the learning strategies when using language. Furthermore, if there is minimal effort and attention to the students while using the strategies it is possible for the learner to receive back the strategy, evaluate, and get the attention needed. In the long-term theory, most information is stored as indicated by the cognitive theory as either procedural knowledge or declarative knowledge.

VanPatten, B., & Williams, J. (2015). *Theories in second language acquisition: An introduction.* **New York : Routledge**

The book supports the idea of the different forms of language learning through explanation of the different strategies. The book introduces the memory strategy whereby it indicates that it is the ability for a person to memorize faster during his or her studies. However, it is easier for an individual to create a word meaning map in their brain which will assist them in remembering in long term memory and also retrieve the information (VanPatten & Williams, 2015). By accepting memory strategy one should accept the retrieval and learning through sound for example images and rhyming, body movement, combination of images and sounds and mechanical means.

Butler, Y. G., & Hakuta, K. (January 01, 2008). Bilingualism and Second Language Acquisition. 114-144.

The author also talks of the comprehensive strategy that involves individuals finding themselves guessing words that are unknown when reading or listening. To overcome gaps in their knowledge they replace words that they do not comprehend with other words or phrases when writing or speaking (Butler & Hakuta, 2008). The author also introduces the Metacognitive strategy whereby a person is capable to evaluate, arrange, focus and plan through his or her own concept of learning. They are used in the identification and monitoring of their personal needs and preferences in learning style.

Brown, H. D. (2007). *Principles of language learning and teaching.* **White Plains, NY: Pearson Longman.**

According to the author, there are different tools that can be used in teaching language. One of the tools if the Corpora. The author indicates that in the early stage, it is advantageous if one learns the most commonly used words in a language. Corpora have also been beneficial to the society since it has been used in the establishment of the reference works and the dictionary for example Collins Cobuild series, published by HarperCollins. In a language, corpora can be useful in identifying the regular words used by native speakers (Brown, 2007). From the corpora patterns teachers are able to teach their learners the second language learning vocabulary.

Leaver, B. L., Ehrman, M. E., & Shekhtman, B. (2005). *Achieving success in second language acquisition.* **Cambridge, UK: Cambridge University Press.**

The book indicates that there are various of attaining success in teaching a second language. It supports the previous authors through indicating that language learning there are numerous methods used in the assessment of the students. Based on the various nature of the student it is beneficial for one to adapt on the variety. The authors also indicate that teachers of the language should be conscious of the students personality and behaviors as to improve their learning strategies. Moreover, in various strategies and learning styles teachers are capable to use variety of assessments and activities methods that would suit their students (Leaver, Ehrman & Shekhtman, 2005). In addition, the move that is well celebrated and encourage is the use of compute in teaching the students. A proper combination of these tools should be operational through an effective language teaching and learning. It is identified that there is no any superior strategy when learning the language and that are various strategies that assist in learning. If there is increase in the occurrence of strategy, the score will not be low range or medium.

Haywood, A. L. (2005). The relationship between student learning styles and L2 acquisition in two international high schools' english language classrooms in Jeddah, Saudi Arabia. Thesis (Ph. D.): University of Mississippi

The paper is a thesis from the University of Mississippi indicating some of the limitations associated with the second language learning. According the author, one of the limitation associates to strategies whereby there is no strategy that is conducive for everyone. Therefore, different personalities receive different strategies. Based on the research it clarifies for one to be a most effective learner and maximize the learning he or she should be better in the use of mixing strategies.

Zhonggen, Y. (April 01, 2016). The Impact of the E-Collaborative and Traditional Learning Styles on Learning Outcomes and Anxiety. *International Journal of E-Collaboration (ijec), 12,* **2,** 27-47.

The author in the article indicates that the teaching strategies that are used might interfere with the learning. The teacher might find it challenging to use every strategy in a class setting even when given resources and time. However, suggestions came across that teachers should at least find away to know few strategies that will involve each of the students despite their opposing personalities. To the different strategies, it is essential for the learners to adapt to the lessons to make it much easier for the teachers as they tutor them in a class setting (Zhonggen, 2016). For instance if a learner identifies that his or her strategies are not catered for he or she has the right to select the strategies that are favorable to him or her by revising and practicing the language with his or her peers. It is easy to indicate that personality is changeable through time and circumstance. Despite that our personality still takes part in the effectiveness of the language learning.

References

Brown, H. D. (2007). *Principles of language learning and teaching.* White Plains, NY: Pearson Longman.

Butler, Y. G., & Hakuta, K. (January 01, 2008). Bilingualism and Second Language Acquisition. 114-144.

Georgetown University Round Table on Languages and Linguistics, & Alatis, J. E. (2010). *Linguistics, language teaching, and language acquisition: The interdependence of theory, practice, and research.* Washington, D.C: Georgetown University Press.

Griffiths, C., & İnceçay, G. (June 01, 2016). Styles and Style-Stretching: How are They Related to Successful Learning?. *Journal of Psycholinguistic Research, 45,* 3, 599-613.

Haywood, A. L. (2005). *The relationship between student learning styles and L2 acquisition in two international high schools' english language classrooms in Jeddah, Saudi Arabia.* Thesis (Ph. D.): University of Mississippi

Leaver, B. L., Ehrman, M. E., & Shekhtman, B. (2005). *Achieving success in second language acquisition.* Cambridge, UK: Cambridge University Press.

Mirzaee, S., & Maftoon, P. (December 01, 2016). An examination of Vygotsky's socio-cultural theory in second language acquisition: the role of higher order thinking enhancing techniques and the EFL learners' use of private speech in the construction of reasoning. *Asian-pacific Journal of Second and Foreign Language Education, 1,* 1, 1-25.

Piper, T. (2011). *And then there were two: Children and second language learning.* Toronto: Pippin Pub.

Purpura, J. E. (January 01, 2016). Second and Foreign Language Assessment. *The Modern Language Journal, 100,* 190-208.

VanPatten, B., & Williams, J. (2015). *Theories in second language acquisition: An introduction.* New York : Routledge

Zhonggen, Y. (April 01, 2016). The Impact of the E-Collaborative and Traditional Learning Styles on Learning Outcomes and Anxiety. *International Journal of E-Collaboration (ijec), 12,* 2, 27-47.

YOUR KNOWLEDGE HAS VALUE

- We will publish your bachelor's and master's thesis, essays and papers

- Your own eBook and book - sold worldwide in all relevant shops

- Earn money with each sale

Upload your text at www.GRIN.com and publish for free